OLIVER KNUSSEN

Whitman Settings

Op 25

(1991)

for soprano and piano

FABER *ff* MUSIC

© 1993 by Faber Music Ltd
First published in 1993 by Faber Music Ltd
3 Queen Square London WC1N 3AU
Music processed by Silverfen
Cover design by S & M Tucker
Printed in England by Halstan & Co Ltd
All rights reserved

ISBN 0 571 51409 X

Whitman Settings was commissioned by the Amphion Foundation

The first performance the first three songs was given by Lucy Shelton and Ian Brown
in the Maltings, Snape as part of the 44th Aldeburgh Festival on 17 June 1991.
The first complete performance was given by Lucy Shelton and John Constable
at BBC Pebble Mill, Birmingham on 15 October 1991

Duration: 12 minutes

Whitman Settings is recorded by Lucy Shelton and Peter Serkin
on Virgin Classics VC 7 59308 2 (CD)

for Lucy Shelton

1. When I Heard the Learn'd Astronomer

When I heard the learn'd astronomer,
When the proofs, the figures, were ranged in columns before
  me,
When I was shown the charts and diagrams, to add, divide, and
  measure them,
When I sitting heard the astronomer where he lectured with
  much applause in the lecture-room,
How soon unaccountable I became tired and sick,
Till rising and gliding out I wander'd off by myself,
In the mystical moist night-air, and from time to time,
Look'd up in perfect silence at the stars.

2. A Noiseless Patient Spider

A noiseless patient spider,
I mark'd where on a little promontory it stood isolated,
Mark'd how to explore the vacant vast surrounding,
It launch'd forth filament, filament, filament, out of itself,
Ever unreeling them, ever tirelessly speeding them.

And you O my soul where you stand,
Surrounded, detached, in measureless oceans of space,
Ceaselessly musing, venturing, throwing, seeking the spheres
  to connect them,
Till the bridge you will need be form'd, till the ductile anchor
  hold,
Till the gossamer thread you fling catch somewhere, O my soul.

3. The Dalliance of the Eagles

Skirting the river road, (my forenoon walk, my rest,)
Skyward in air a sudden muffled sound, the dalliance of the
  eagles,
The rushing amorous contact high in space together,
The clinching interlocking claws, a living, fierce, gyrating wheel,
Four beating wings, two beaks, a swirling mass tight grappling,
In tumbling turning clustering loops, straight downward
  falling,
Till o'er the river pois'd, the twain yet one, a moment's lull,
A motionless still balance in the air, then parting, talons loosing,
Upward again on slow-firm pinions slanting, their separate
  diverse flight,
She hers, he his, pursuing.

4. The Voice of the Rain

And who art thou? said I to the soft-falling shower,
Which, strange to tell, gave me an answer, as here translated:
I am the Poem of Earth, said the voice of the rain,
Eternal I rise impalpable out of the land and the bottomless sea,
Upward to heav'n, whence, vaguely form'd, altogether
       changed, and yet the same,
I descend to lave the drouths, atomies, dust layers of the globe,
And all that in them without me were seeds only, latent,
       unborn;
And forever, by day and night, I give back life to my own
       origin, and make pure and beautify it:
(For song, issuing from its birth-place, after fulfilment,
       wandering,
Reck'd or unreck'd, duly with love returns.)

Walt Whitman (1819-92)

Whitman Settings
for soprano and piano

Walt Whitman
(1819–92)

Oliver Knussen
Op. 25
(1991)

1. When I Heard the Learn'd Astronomer

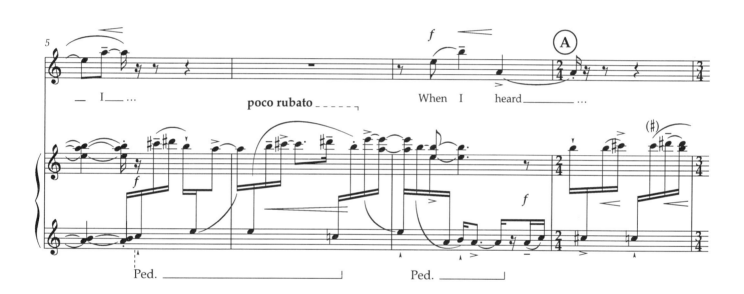

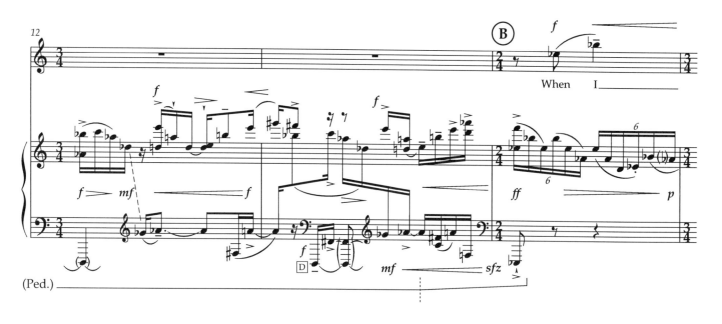

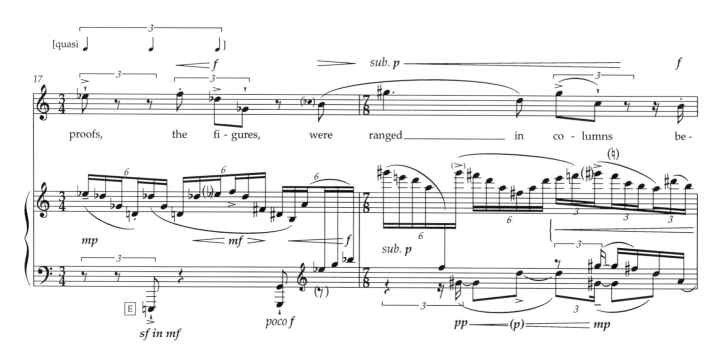

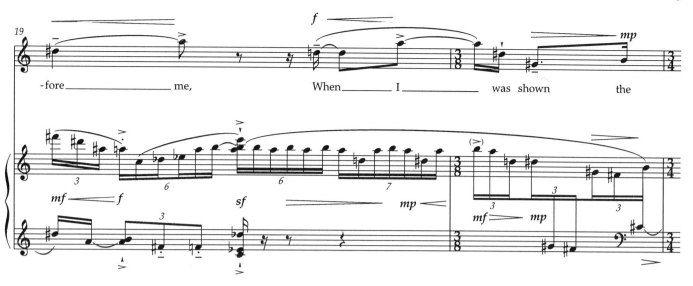

-fore _____ me, When ____ I ____ was shown the

charts and di - a - grams, to add, di-vide, and mea-sure them,

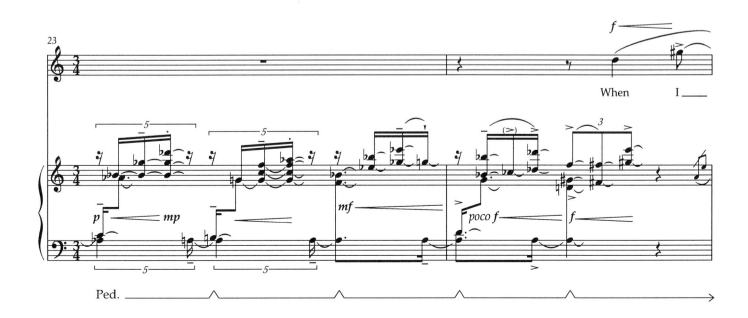

When I ____

Ped.

4

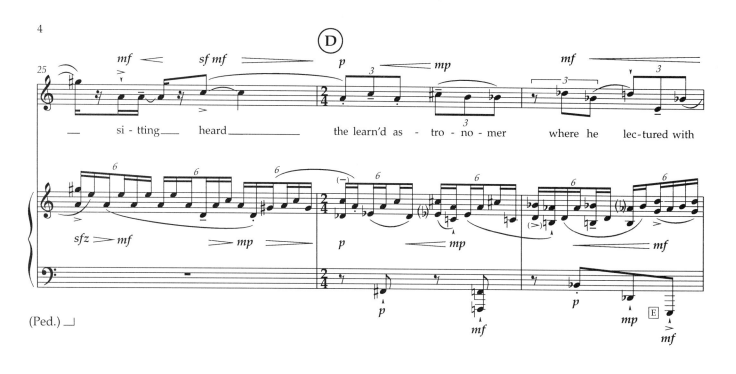

si - tting____ heard____ the learn'd as - tro - no - mer where he lec-tured with

(Ped.) ⌐

much a-pplause_____ in the lec - ture - room,____

Ped. _____

Ⓔ
poco largamente

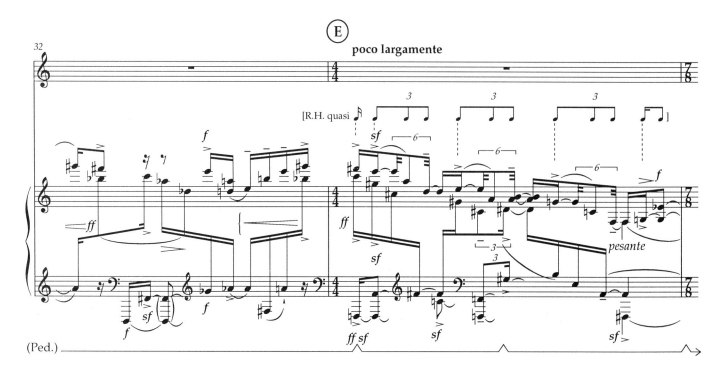

(Ped.) _____

6

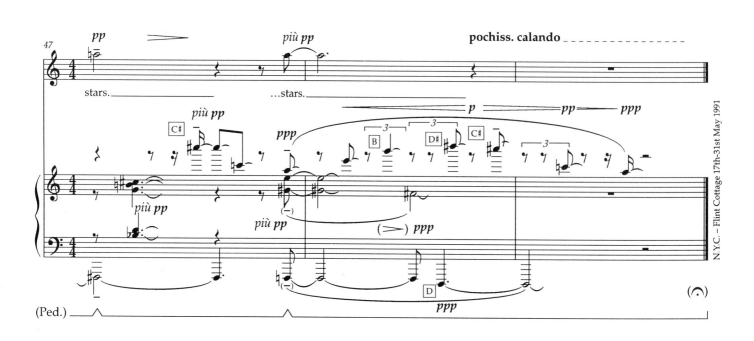

N.Y.C. – Flint Cottage 17th-31st May 1991

2. A Noiseless Patient Spider

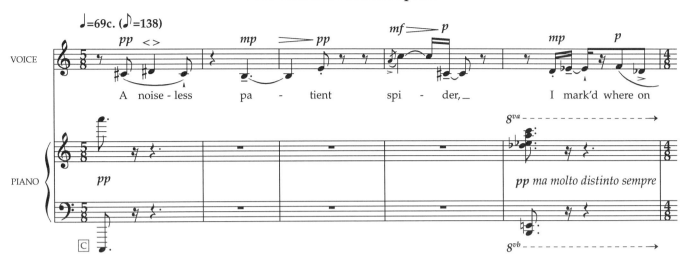

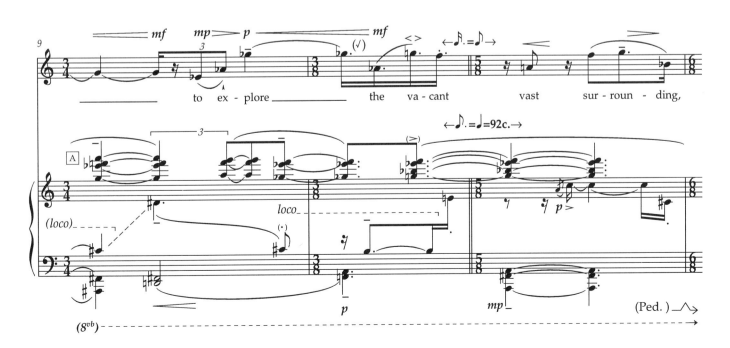

8

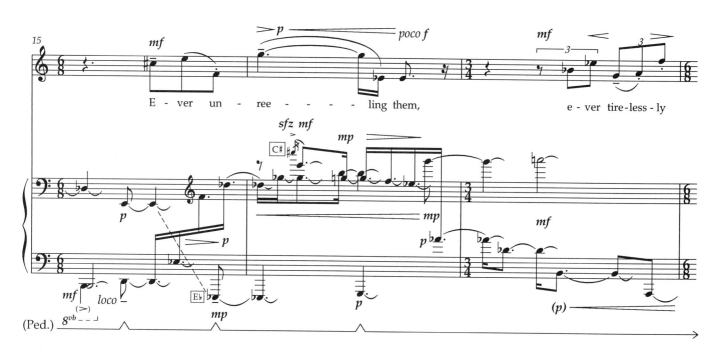

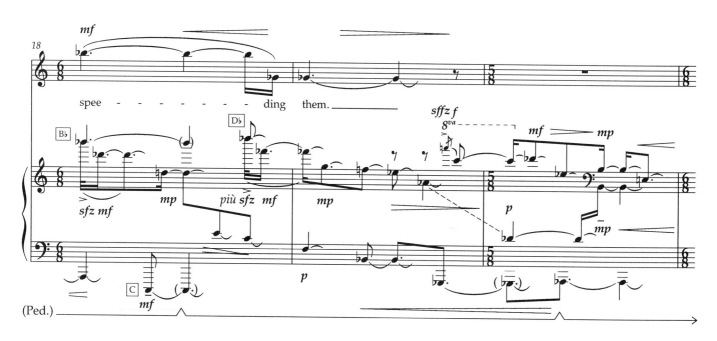

where you stand,

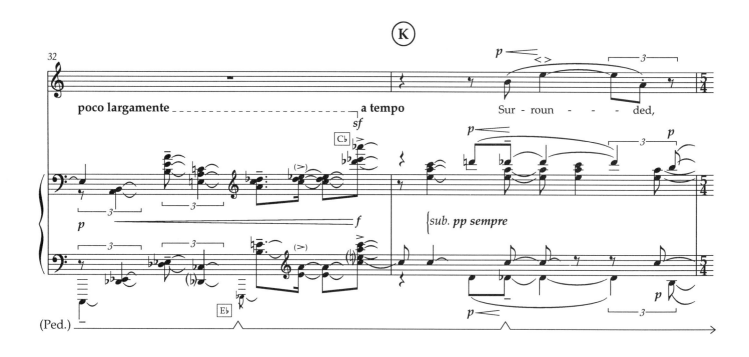

poco largamente _ _ _ _ _ _ _ _ _ _ _ _ a tempo

Sur - roun - - - ded,

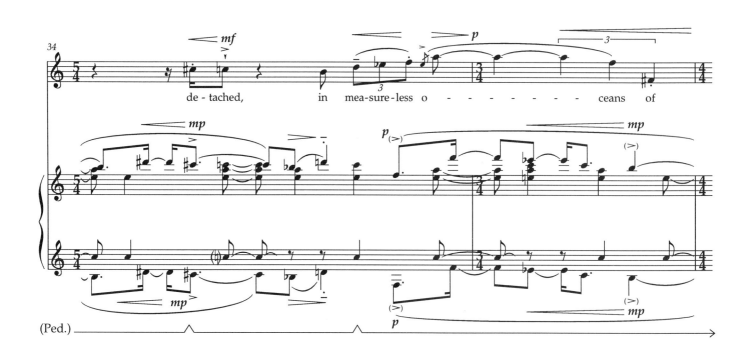

de - tached, in mea-sure-less o - - - - - - ceans of

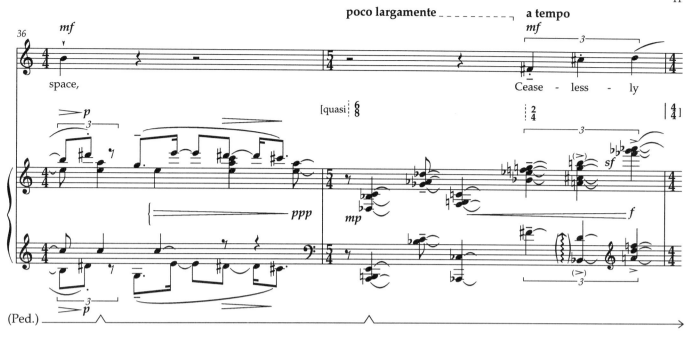

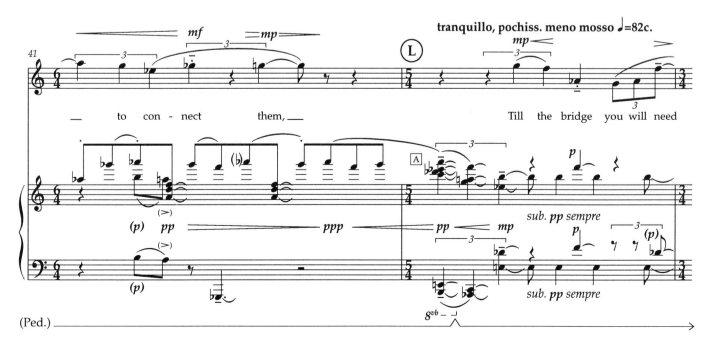

12

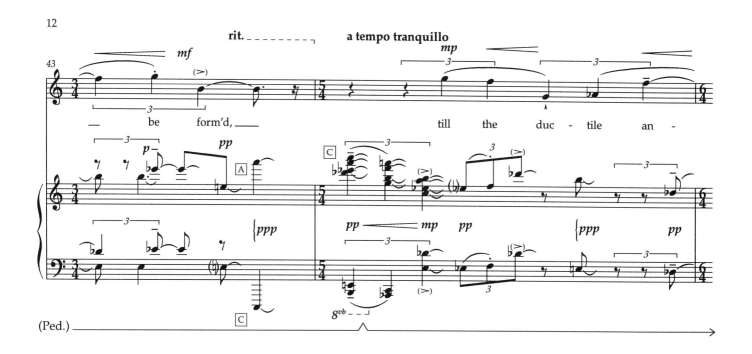

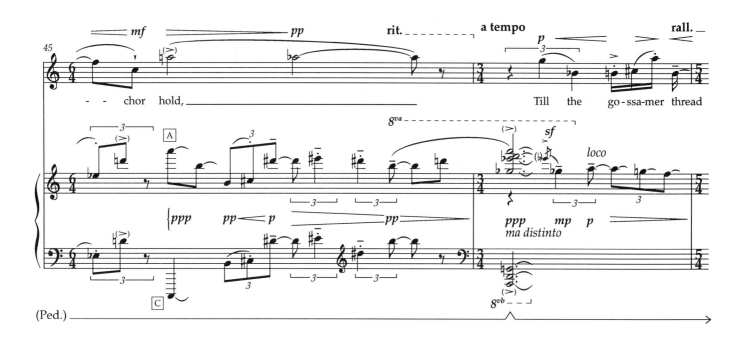

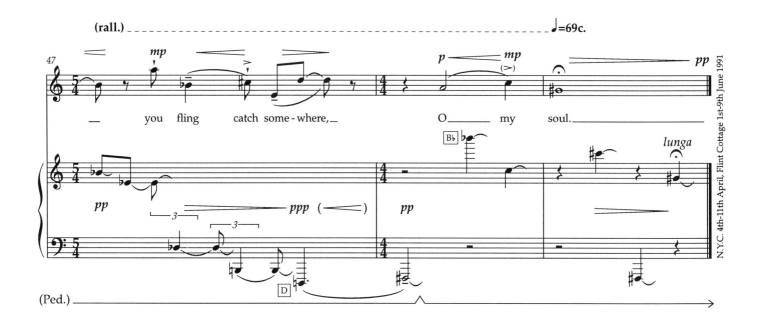

N.Y.C. 4th–11th April, Flint Cottage 1st–9th June 1991

3. The Dalliance of the Eagles

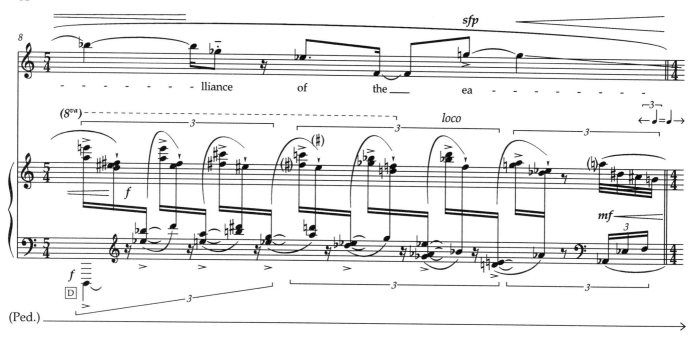

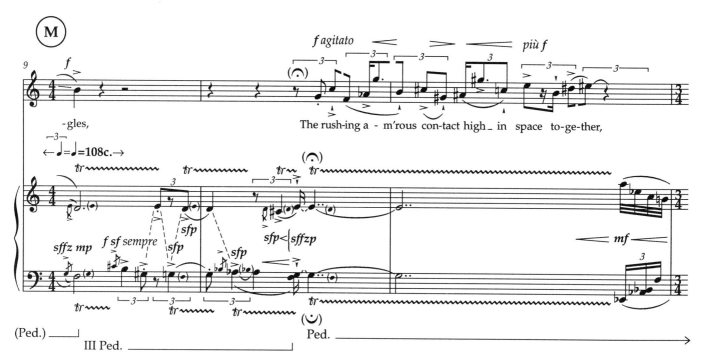

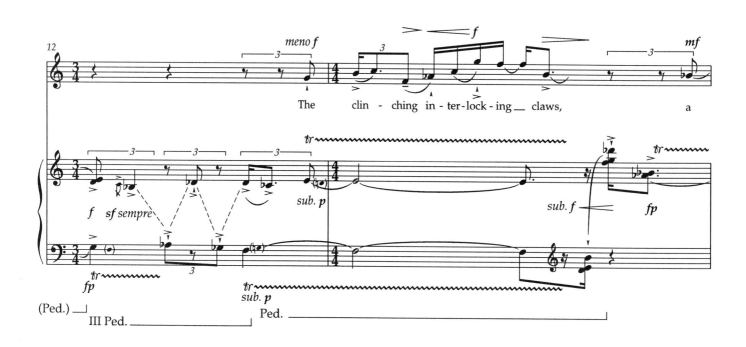

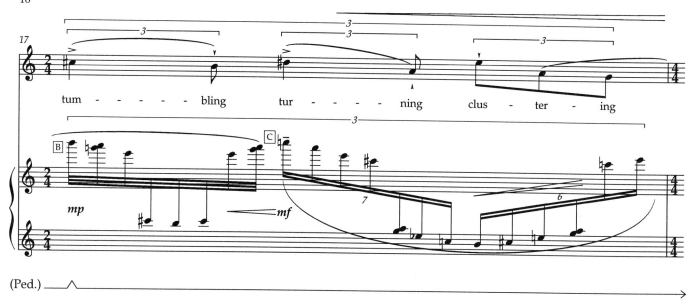

tum - - - - bling   tur - - ning   clus - ter - ing

(Ped.) _____

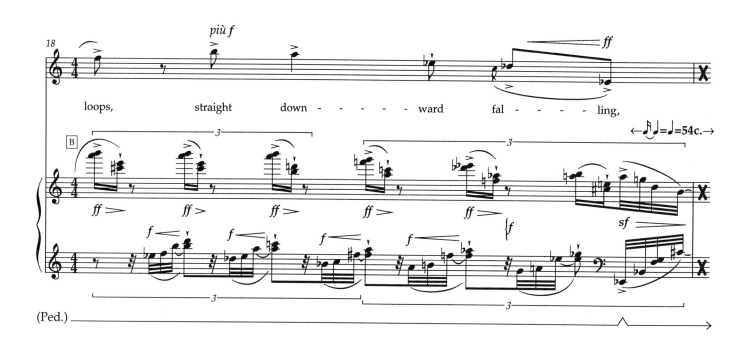

loops,   straight   down - - - - ward   fal - - - ling,

(Ped.) _____

Senza misura ma ben in tempo

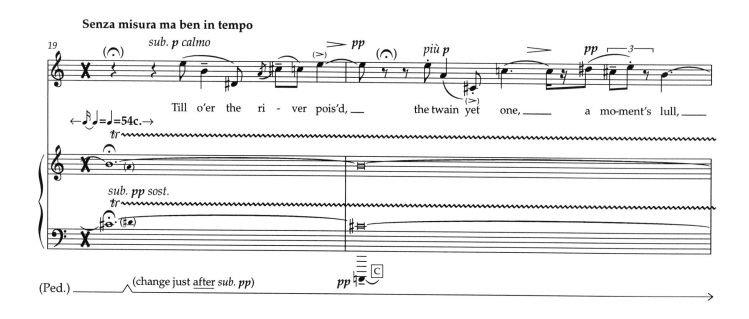

Till o'er the ri - ver pois'd, ___ the twain yet one, ___ a mo-ment's lull, ___

(Ped.) _____ (change just after sub. pp)

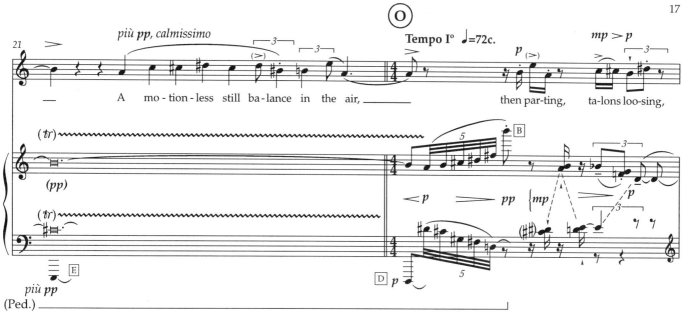

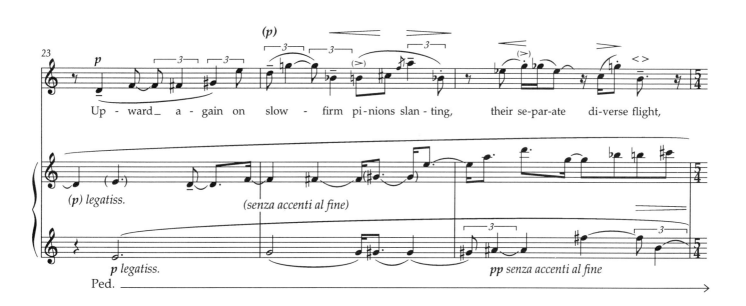

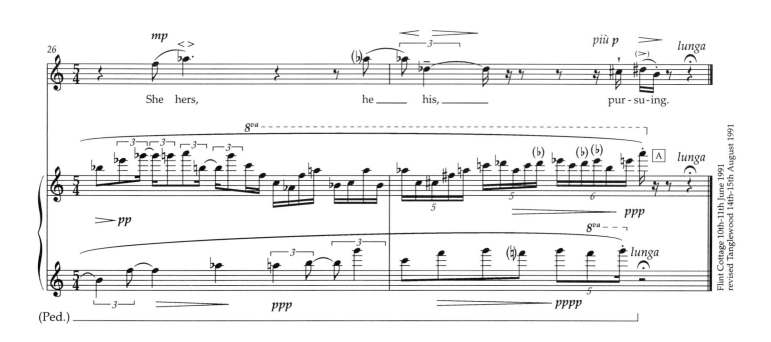

Flint Cottage 10th–11th June 1991
revised Tanglewood 14th–15th August 1991

4. The Voice of the Rain

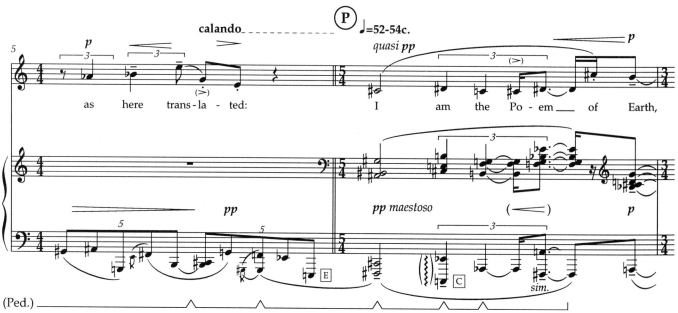

said the voice of the rain, E - ter - nal I

rise im - pal - pa-ble out of the

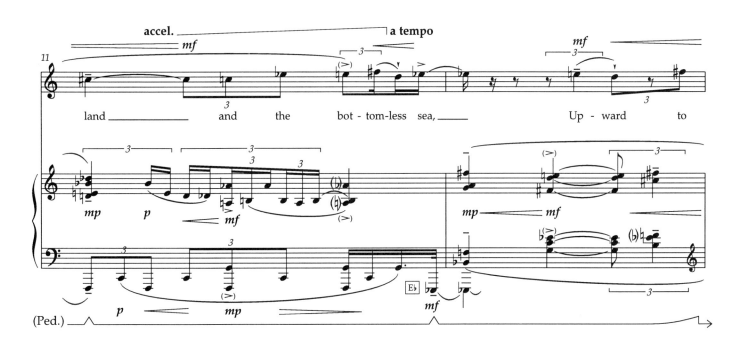

land and the bot - tom-less sea, Up - ward to

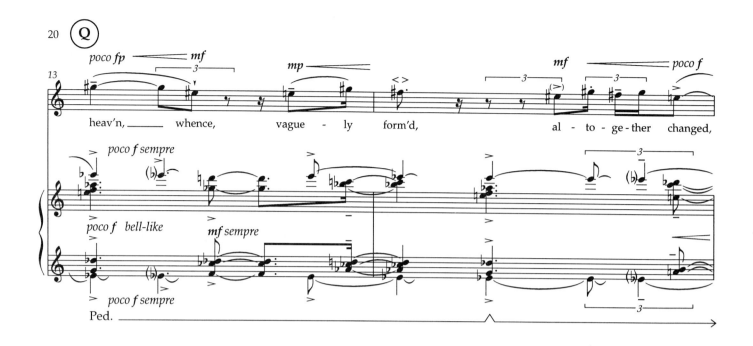

heav'n, _____ whence, vague - ly form'd, al - to - ge - ther changed,

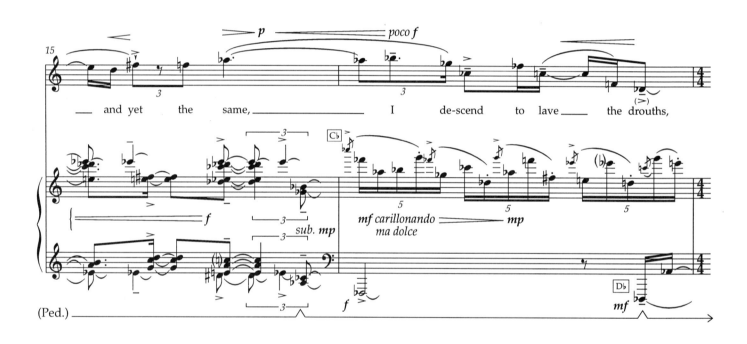

_____ and yet the same, _____ I de-scend to lave _____ the drouths,

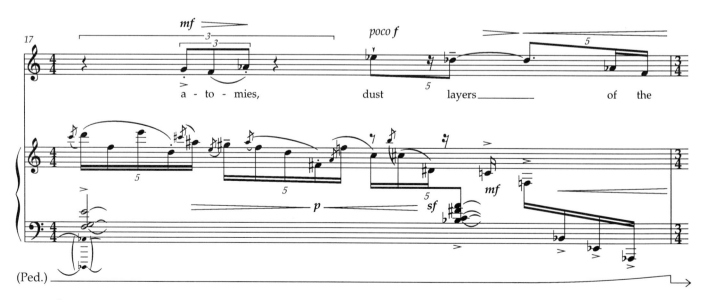

a - to - mies, dust layers_____ of the

* **NB** ♪ here is approximately equal to ♪ at the beginning.

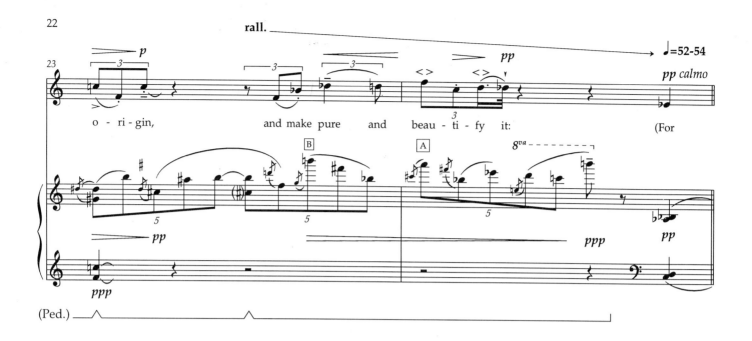

o - ri - gin,   and make pure   and   beau - ti - fy it: (For

song,   iss - uing from its   birth - place,   af - ter ful - fil - ment,   wan - der - ing,

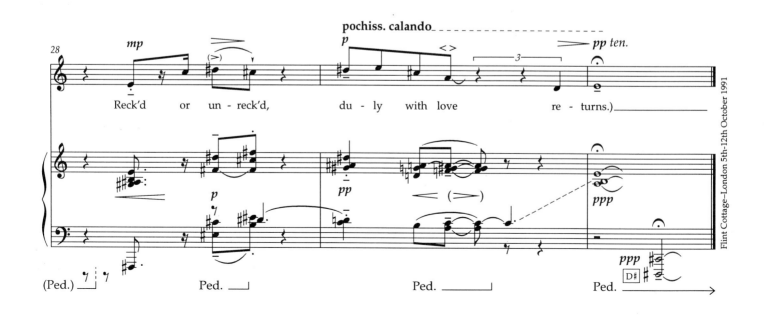

Reck'd   or   un - reck'd,   du - ly   with love   re - turns.)

Flint Cottage—London 5th-12th October 1991